Moving
the
Seasons

Moving the Seasons

Selected Poems of
Charles Guenther

B k M k PRESS

THE UNIVERSITY OF MISSOURI-KANSAS CITY

A C K N O W L E D G M E N T S

Acknowledgment is due to the following publications in which most of these poems have appeared: ALTA Newsletter, The American Poetry Review, Askance, CIV/n (Canada), Curled Wire Chronicle, Driftwind, Eyeball, Gryphon, International Anthology (Greece), The Literary Review, Mademoiselle, Missouri Poets: An Anthology, The Observer, Poet Lore, Poetry Fund Journal, The Slate, St. Louis Literary Supplement, St. Louis Post-Dispatch, Thirteen Poets, Voices From the Interior, Webster Review, Weid, and WWhimsy.

Fourteen poems in this book appeared in a previous collection, Phrase/Paraphrase (Iowa City, IA: The Prairie Press, 1970).

Book Design & Typography by Michael Annis.
Author photo by Charles J. Guenther, Jr.

LIBRARY OF CONGRESS
Library of Congress Cataloging-in-Publication Data

Guenther, Charles, 1920-
  Moving the seasons : selected poems of Charles Guenther /
by Charles Guenther.
    p.   cm.
    ISBN 0-933532-98-9 : $12.00 paper
    I. Title.
PS3557.U32M68   1994
    811'.54—dc20   94-16670
                                                       CIP

Support from the Bernardin/Haskell Funds of the University of Missouri-Kansas City helped make this book possible.

 Financial assistance for this book has been provided by the Missouri Arts Council, a state agency.

Bk Mk PRESS

Dan Jaffe, Director
Rae Furnish, Associate Editor
C. Todd White, Editorial Assistant

For the voices of lost faces

R E F O R M A T I O N S

Charles Guenther's poems, translations, and criticism have appeared in more than 250 different U.S. and foreign magazines. He is the author of six books of poems and translations including *Modern Italian Poets* (1961), *Phrase/Paraphrase* (poems), *Paul Valery in English* (1970), *Voices in the Dark* (1974), and *The Hippopotamus: Selected Translations* (1986). His poetry—as well as his translations from French, Spanish, and Italian—may be found in numerous anthologies such as *New Directions* (20 and 40), *Modern European Poetry* (Bantam Books, 1966), *Roots and Wings* (Harper and Row, 1976), *Voices Within the Ark* (Avon Books, 1980), and *The Sun Dancing* (Penguin, 1982).

In 1973 Charles Guenther received Italy's highest decoration, the Order of Merit of the Italian Republic, in the rank of commander, for his many translations of Italian poetry. He has also won The James Joyce Award of the Poetry Society of America (1974), the Missouri Library Association Literary Award (1974), the French Bicentennial Medal (1976), and in 1979, both the Webster Review translation prize and the Witter Bynner Poetry Translation grant of The Poetry Society of America. In 1981 he received one of three literary fellowships awarded by the St. Louis Arts and Humanities Commission.

Charles Guenther has read and recorded his poetry on scores of campuses throughout the United States and for many campus affiliated and independent radio stations. In 1972 he read and recorded his poetry at the Library of Congress for the Archive of Recorded Poetry and Literature. In May 1967 the Olin Library, Washington University, compiled a 60-page bibliography of his many publications, not including hundreds of newspaper reviews and articles. He has reviewed books of poetry, fiction, and criticism for the St. Louis Post-Dispatch since 1953, and for the St. Louis Globe-Democrat since 1972.

A former government translator, historian, geographer, supervisory cartographer and librarian, he changed careers to teaching in 1975.

INTRODUCTION

As our society drifts toward the derangement of Newspeak, the language of George Orwell's *1984*, it becomes necessary to celebrate the heroes of resistance. We need to struggle to educate the taste and to enlighten the mind. We must resist the forces that make it first purpose to satisfy juvenile demand, that encourage libraries to eliminate first edition collections to provide space for videos, that urge universities to dump the classics in favor of computers. That's why we need to focus on figures like Charles Guenther, a man who stands for the light of literature, for the daring of the imagination, for the pursuit of craft, and for the belief in great achievement wherever it can be found.

Charles understands the democratic nature of greatness. He knows that the subtle and difficult achievement, which at first glance may seem elitist because it is so rare, is like Lincoln or Jefferson or George Washington Carver, so aptly named. Though truly uncommon they provided great gifts to us all. Such greatness is democratic in another sense as well. It can be found anywhere: in the smallest town in Missouri, in the metropolis, in the barrio or in the mansion. It can express itself in the King's English or in languages you have never heard of. The great writers can be Welsh or Ugandan, Egyptian or German, French or Native American, Israeli or Swedish. Think of their names, great ones like Twain or Rilke, Yeats or Cavafy, Amichai or Hughes, Shakespeare, Dante, and Li Po, to mention a few. Yes, they wrote for themselves but for all of us as well. To appreciate them we need to be able to read more than forms and signs and work directions; we need to be able to reach outside of ourselves.

Let me ask: What shall we say of a man who has given his life to the pursuit of letters at the highest level, who has taught and translated, who has made his own poems, who "whittled a style from a walnut stick," to quote Archibald Macleish? What shall we say of this private man who has regularly devoted his life to the public discussion of other writers' work?

Charles Guenther may not be a name known to the general public. It is likely that most puny politicians will have greater name recognition. But I say let Charles Guenther be our model rather than some purveyor of jargon or economic promises. Why? Because he has worked to keep the basic tool of our personal and social understanding, the language, sharp. He has insisted we have the capacity to hear it, to use it, and to appreciate it.

You don't need a vita sheet to value the power in Charles Guenther's gentle voice. Remember what he stands for: the elegance of the honest line; the achievement of precise articulation; the need for the unique perspective; the wonder of deep connections between words and people.

These comments are of course inadequate. The dimensions of a man's achievement in a lifetime cannot be captured in an introduction. Only a great poem might release such meanings, which is the real point, the point Charles Guenther has devoted his life to.

Charles Guenther's poems and translations, or "reformations" as he prefers to call them, reveal considerable technical skills. They also show his great humility, his devotion to the reader and to other writers of merit as well. Above all, he is a man who weighs his words.

—Dan Jaffe

I

P O E M S

The Current

The sluggish current
                    of the river
          won't carry off
                    a bundle of thorns
     Brothers   we are
          Don't believe
          what men say
               they lie

The sluggish current
                    of the river
          won't carry away
                    a bundle of wood
     Brothers   we'll remain
          only you and I
               Don't rely
          on what others say
               rumors and lies

— From *Notes From a Journey*

Horses

My lord's horses
                    clatter and rumble
          his suit
               is the color of reeds
     How can I forget you?
                         But I fear him

My lord's horses
                    clatter and rumble
          his coat
               is heavy with rubies
     How can I forget you?
                         But I'm terrified
          I can't even walk
               into the meadow

Living we sleep
                    in separate rooms
Dead we'll sleep
               together
     If you believe
                    I am unfaithful
          the sun is my witness

North Wind

The north wind
                    blows cold
        rain, snow, squalls
            O tenderly
            hold my hand
                let's go
        if you love me
                    why wait
        the time has come

The north wind
                        blows up a storm
        rain, snow, whirlwinds
            O tenderly
            hold my hand
                let's go
        if you love me
                    why wait
        the time is now

Nothing's so red as a fox
                        or black as a crow
            O tenderly
            hold my hand
                let's ride off together
        if you love me
                    why wait
        our time has come

Kinds of Love (i)

A stranger told me something about you
I didn't know. I bent an ear
pretending to be indifferent, impervious
to gossip, but the shallow
secret struck me like a blade. Why
didn't you tell me? It's a commonplace
thing. Did you think I knew? Did you care
if I knew? These questions
may never be answered, and the fragment
of fact lie forever
heavy between us.

Kinds of Love (ii)

He and she are absent: only we,
you and I are here; we are named.
                                    You aren't she
but you, never anything else. Others
will speak of you against my wishes, but
what others say of you will not be you.

For a Friend Unjustly Maligned

A Job struck by infinite
pain will manifest
his grief and only fears it
won't faze us in the least.
When we see his plight,
the open sores, the bed of pains,
we'd better get used to the sight:
a man suffers and complains.

While he's hurt and still endures
incredible agonies,
plagues without cures,
we've seen patience exceed his:
he groused about his tortures.
You knew much worse than these.

E.E.C.*

E.E. would have given us
the roof of his treehouse
(the better to see the
    " s   k   y ")

let no one trespass there
to take from his Nature
for man-ready rifles
make man-loving neighbors

No painter of unmyths
he knew realistic
alias "anecdotal"
was NOT legal tender

nor was nonobjective
alias "abstract"
both MIScalled "art"
(two sides of the same coin)

the man of good humor
of tulips and chimneys
whose art was a question
of being alive

looked forward to back
a most meaningful birth
until a red tide
freed a miraculous flood

*"*Thank you for asking if I want my name in lower case:
no, I do not.*"—Letter, January 17,'58.*

From "A Room at St. Anthony's"

(To Sister M. Crescentia)

XVIII

Westphalia
Kahle Asten the sugar cone
and the dark-pointed pines
Nuhne ice-crusted
        the double Advent
Hallenberg   Liesen
Paderborn
Solingen
to Dortmund and Witten
and Olpe
having spent nine contented years

Nine brown habits
nine black scapulars
nine white cords
        a pearly song broke the silence

Ora Labora
seed and fruit

In a barn at Salzkotten
breakfast was bread and black coffee
supper thin soup and dry bread
and no fats at midday
        despite the Bishop's concern

Young girls soon begged admittance
and served on the Bohemian battlefields
for the Queen's praise
then the Kulturkampf
and the nine months at Wesel
        and the five sisters
           drowned
           (O soft sift
        in an hourglass)

De Profundis
De Profundis
De Profundis
De Profundis
De Profundis

        (Deo Gratias)

A mandate and secret
plenary power
to accept and invest
to administer
to accept and discontinue

Nine and nineteen
postulants invested
        Bad Schwalbach
        and the seven seals   the flames of fire
        and the lips
            pressed together
in pace

L' Homme des Chats

(for A. J. Montesi)

When Peter Bently tooled around in his cream-
colored Stutz Bearcat 90 years ago,
was it only a fiction, Al Montesi's dream?
Think whatever you want, but I'd say no.

To begin: we must consider all the formal
truths—the time, the place (historical facts)
and the credibility of a cat named Carmel,
a bird named Blackie, a German shepherd Max.

I know. I've been through four American wars,
driven a Whippet, ridden a Moon and Stars.
Montesi: a poet, scholar, mentor, friend,

all that remains are the best years to use;
today's like any other, it isn't the end
of anything. Take them, savor them as you choose.

The Language Machine

Or, On First Looking Into Edmundson's *Proceedings of the National Symposium on Machine Translation*

After the scholars cull the homographs
Dismembering words by function (complex and plain)
Marking the beginning and end of paragraphs
Sentences quotes on sheets of cellophane
The format is established units fit
By text and context separate verbs that mean
One value syllables letters all of it
Goes into code and is fed in the machine
(Beast that needs and takes no breaks or lunches)
Which punches sorts prints punches sorts
Prints punches punches punches sorts
Sorts sorts prints prints prints
Punches punches punches

Instant Sonnet

A colleague sent an order for a sonnet.
"Lucky devil!" you say. ("Poor ange-
l" is more like it.) But I've put three lines on it;
not only that, I've contrived a rhyme for "orange."
The secret's in doing the words one by one,
making it line by line, stave by stave,
and before you know it, it's already half done.
Add another line and you've finished the octave.

Enter the sestet with more confidence
and now we've only four more lines to go;
mold it spare, unpadded, give it sense,
then drain the couplet like honey poured slow-
ly from a cup, its substance long extended,
for suddenly this living exercise is ended.

Tenson

(with commentary)

Poeta, volontieri
Parlerei a quei due che'nsemo vanno.
—Inferno V

J'étais obscur au simple populaire;
Mais on dit aujourd'hui que je suis au contraire.
—Ronsard

Take a straight song Shun
circuit diluted wine
See the immodest sun
yield the strongest line—

Giraut who would forbear
poetry of the dark
dropped such a remark
adding upon the clear

—Sleep or be understood
Raimbaut you claim too hard
applause of the multitude
rime's only **reward**

But Raimbaut interposed
("virtuoso of form"
to whom legend supposed
Beatrix was warm)

—What if my song's not
thrown to the ends of the earth
is there any sot
can judge it what it's worth

No abundant dish
is ever delicate
Giraut—Damn me if you wish
I've salt on my plate
.   .   .

As Marcellus Giraut
overweeningly
indiscreet let go
praise of the Maccabees

though "a count's equal"
provoked a reprimand
from her he courted and
saw her buckler turn
                    The sequel

to Bernart the scullion for
he had loved Agnes
                    Caught
by the viscount he sought
tutelage of Eleanore

Guillem de Cabestanh
the countess Seremonde
loved ate his heart atoned
(relics at Perpignan)

And knave Guillem to whom
with mysterious pride
a trobairitz replied
All Provence knew the doom

of heretic chatelains
(but think of indigo-
eyed Lucinda's profane
commanded fandango)

Sing sing the prince of Blaye
sing Rousillon who ran
ruefully
Dan dan
dan deridan deridan dei

Silences

The last words fall gently as a closing of blinds.
All we can say of freedom merely restrains it. No
instant or object, nor the events of your unleashing
heart can be measured beside you. Absent you are
present: our mouths share the wind.

When the living day disappears silence vacillates
in the amber gardens. Flowers breathe colors. (We
have already plucked the lilac of the tempest.) Sleep
joyfully to the sound of the sun on your blue island
of other silences. There is no festival but here.

Three Sisters

i. Sara Pondering
(on *Sara Teasdale and Vachel Lindsay*)

Maybe it was some power in him you feared
as he went about trading his rhymes for sustenance,
an unbroken bronco whose exuberance
broke at last when his hope and fortune disappeared,

or maybe it was the fiery evangelist
in him, the visionary hustler of empty schemes,
or the carnival prophet hawking impractical dreams
or the missionary poet, the ragtime rhapsodist?

—all these perhaps.

                As we'd mistrust some wild
dark of the woods or an unknown deep of the sea,
your taming spirit couldn't be reconciled

to the eagle in him you admired flying free
into the sun where together alike are lost
your August rain and his November frost.

ii. Remembering Marianne

(on letters from Marianne Moore, April 1962)

When I asked if the house I'd lived in was your same
childhood home and described it: the long antique
veranda, 1840s, cisterns, frame
now stuccoed yellow and tiled, where a stony little creek

trickled through a wild orchard of red plums
and a field of dewberries — you didn't say.
(Still
our separate worlds were linked by the chromosomes,
as you called them, of each clustered syllable.)

Those years I took circuitous roads to truth,
ignored your hints, suggested even doing a "feature"
on you, but patiently you'd shrug and sluff

it off, saying, "I'm not important enough,"
adding, "Eliot is ideal."

We'll forget the architecture,
but I know I tasted those wild plums of your youth.

iii. Conjuring H.D.: A Year with Richard
(on Hilda Doolittle and Richard Aldington)

They say there is no hope / to conjure you
(How curious to read your lines at the rim
of a sonnet)
                    Yet in a beech that shudders through
its leaves you were trembling and still to him:

a blossom shaken by the wind, a swirl
of startled sparrows flushed, an autumn mist
lingering in the woods or a lonely curl
of smoke in an evening dark as amethyst

—you were all these.
                    For when the spirit sum-
mons spirit, how to tell its strange embrace?
Is the reflection truth? Is it the cold

face of a lotus pool or is it the face
of flesh?
              No matter the image, young or old,
you have become in these. Now you've become.

Attachments

The idea of man in space is fascinating:
over the atmosphere, thinner in relation
to the earth than an appleskin, he arched
from reality into mystery,
free in his motion, weightless.
                              In his vertical thrust
he lost all adhesion and
became immobile, until he contrived
cabins of artificial gravity.
He missed, you see, his attachments, a primitive
need at once obsessed him to hold fast
to something, for he didn't know
if he could cling to anything beyond.

The Chase

The hare and the tortoise,
the hound and the fox,

they have in common
a fading ratio.

Yet, to lumber after a fine hare,
to lope after a sleek fox!

But the hard hills,
the mischief of winter!

Not even a ribbon
consoles; the race

an hallucination
of radiant encounters.

Only when we gather
the highest figs

from the highest branches
do we notice the stars,

and we ask what happened
to make the lightning

vanish, without remembering
when the chase is ended

the prize we wanted
or the one that mattered.

Counterpoem

As we lie on the grass
let's watch the sky,
read its face like a clock's
and study the clouds.

Some are sheep,
common animals
browsing on unseen stars
day after brilliant day,
stars never consumed.

Sometimes we search for the sheep
only to find they've become
giant hills, balloons
or a soldier prone in the sky.

Wholly detached from the earth,
mushrooms suddenly rise.

Missouri Woods

Post oak, white oak, black oak, Ozark rails,
shake roofs and fences split with maul and froe:
remember the timberland, the vanished trails

Laid, lapped and panelled, propped or locked with nails,
the zigzag fences stretching row on row —
post oak, white oak, black oak, Ozark rails.

Tables and staves and dishes, pitch-lined pails
curled from a blade and fashioned long ago,
remember the timberland, the vanished trails.

Cradles and coffins, rafts loaded with bales,
bolts, blocks and pickets, handles for hammer and hoe;
post oak, white oak, black oak, Ozark rails,

logs hollowed for john boats, poles for paddles and sails —
their stubble and stumps poke up the crusted snow.
(Remember the timberland, the vanished trails?)

The blown out nest, the branch that cracks and fails
are lost from the land where only the birds know.
Post oak, white oak, black oak, Ozark rails:
remember the timberland, the vanished trails.

Ste. Genevieve: Memorial Cemetery

The children find a game among the stones,
Searching for dates on them under the heavy trees;
Oak, pine and dark-fruited mulberries
Whose roots embrace and are nourished by the bones
Of the Vallés and the Roziers and the Linns.
A holiday. The town has sealed itself from the heat
Or gravitates to a park across the street,
Just within view, where a carnival begins

With a crash of popular music: visible lives
Divisible. Here by the spider and the mold
Children stop to eat mulberries. Blue and gold,
The day presents its trophies. The bee thrives.
The seasons' wheel gyrates and disappears
And memory withers from memorable acts,
Stripped to pairs of inconsequential facts
Sunk in a tended lawn for the pioneers.

You aren't mine, gentle people, except through the womb
Of Eve: infants, couples who took your vows
Together, but I love your coolness in the boughs.
Seasons are shadows whose continuum
Is to die. But how life flourishes there
For the silent, invisible, indivisible dead
In a corner of shade we think uninhabited,
Since no swan cries in this monumental air.

Father's Memorials

When I was a boy Kingshighway Memorial Boulevard
was the same broad avenue it is today:
double-deck buses ran its length from Gravois
to Florissant, the public schools stadium
had just been built.
                    My sister and I would ramble
over there and peer through the iron railings
at football games until some kindly old coach
of thirty or so gave us free passes, and
Mother admonished us for wandering off so far.
I was seven. "Old Ironsides" played at the Bridge
starring Esther Ralston; Harold Lloyd drove a tram
in "Speedy," and Laurel and Hardy had been born.

Earlier, for the first time in my life
I trembled at music when "The Stars and Stripes
Forever" resounded from a live marching band
down Lindell Boulevard on a hot June day,
a city ecstatic welcoming Lindy home.

Then the city fathers decided to remember
hundreds of doughboys who perished in the war
(the Great War to end all wars and make the world
safe for democracy), each commemorated
with name, rank, branch of service, proper dates
on a bronze marker set under a sapling,
twin rows of plane trees down the divider strip
from Easton to Penrose on the boulevard
which rivaled, it was hoped, the boulevards of Paris
and honored for eternity all those
gassed, killed in the trenches, lost at sea
or shot down over France and Germany.

The plantings flourished and greened through the Depression
to the next war, shading the anxieties
of motorists who pooled day after day
to offices and factories. Birds sang in the branches.

Now 65 years and four American wars
later, the markers gradually have disappeared
one by one, potholes dot the road
like craters on a pitted battlefield, the trees
are stripped and ravaged by storms, only a nuisance
of fallen limbs and leaves.
                              Yet soon even these
great trunks too will be shattered or felled, rivaling
the desolation of Verdun, the surrogate
life of the dead become a regiment of stumps
like headstones tumbled in an old park where nothing
is meant to be remembered, or meant to be forgotten.

Union Station

Only the swallows circling these cones of silence
Make this their hostel now. Their invisible track
Circumscribes a valley where ancient springs
Flowed from the western hills before the air
Droned with wheels by the dam and the artificial pool
In the mills that stood near the gorge where Rock Creek ends.

How the face of the valley changes! One thing ends,
Replaced by another with intervals of silence:
Once there was a prairie with scrub oak, an occasional pool
Where buffalo grazed and drank, their tumbling track
Mistaken for thunder shook the morning air.
Flushing out every creature that flies or springs.

Yet who knows how many thousands of springs
The same scenario plays before it ends,
How many upheavals of earth and air
Hold no recollection in postludes of silence;
Only a beetle perhaps, inscribing its track
Patiently, returns to the edge of an obscure pool.

And here the Osage camped where the bed of the pool
Lay, settlers came for the pure springs
And the black earth, mountain men left to track
Deer and beaver from where the Missouri ends
Up to its headwaters in the lands of silence,
And boatmen labored and danced to some old French air.

Under cedars and cottonwoods, ghosts in the moonlit air.
Lovers pressed on the grass by the glassy pool
(Where have they gone? Only a winter silence
Lies with the faded stones by the vanished springs).
The valley reclaimed, the pond was drained to the ends
Of its arms and coves to lay the parallel track,

Nineteen miles of tentacular steel track!
Gray stones and Spanish tiles, spires in the air,
Rose over the roundhouse where the landscape ends,
Apex and terminus once of a human pool
That swarmed to the coupled cars with the well-oiled springs,
Where rolling stock stands here rusting in silence.

In the lace of a trestle and track, a sunken pool,
Honeysuckle hangs in the air: a new life springs
Until everything ends once more in the music of silence.

ΛRCH

Founder of stone open now to all O Pierre O
Auguste of Pain Court log cabins Levee men labored on
hot summer afternoons and hauled flour and furs over
the muddy uncobbled riverbank or in winter cold cut
ice from the water as puffing packets whirled soot
upward into blue air and trains hooted tooted & went
clang!

Gaslit silver & gold chandeliered purple-draped
palaces of gray busts & brocades are gone O Eero but
your ARCH rose a hero's window on a court of
freedom falling or rising Elk-coated Lewis & Clark's
little town — palisaded & river-facing turned around
to west meeting mirroring the married streams Jacob's
Manuel's (O sage traders) fortunes rocketing Risen out
of flames or plague you flourished and grew Bellefon-
taine & south into Carondelet and west a jewel-park
shimmering structures So proudly open your steel gate
St. Louis!

USA / 50

"America is alone: many together" —A. *MacLeish*

1

What winds blown from old countries carried west
Eric, Lief (Eric's son) and all the rest,
Captains and navigators from Moguer,
Outcasts, conquistadores to spoil the flower
Of the New World! Vinland to Peru,
Fruit of the Indies filled their caravels:

It was a paradise—Ponce de Leon's—
Palms, flamingoes, flying fish, the sun
Shafting the swamps.
                    It was De Soto's too:
Beautiful as a cane box full of pearls,
Espíritu Santo to the Apalachi,
North and west, Tocaste, Napateca,
Blue butterflies, plumed warriors in canoes,
Tokens of love: Mochila, Macanoche.

Come, bearded rider, sleep in the belly of the stream:
The peel-fish take you, the barbel and the bream.

2

Sails slackened on the shoals:
                    Virginia!
White cranes flew up to the high cedars,
Granganimo, the copper-capped, the king

Of bows and arrows, jungle villages strode
Lands of blue grapes and mortar-beaten corn;
And smoke was sucked from the embers of burned weeds.

Pasonagessit revelry: Priapus
And Proteus in the host of Merry Mount,
Morton and his Maypole and his beer-

Mad bacchanalians gamboling on the green;
And Cotton Mather's wonders: witches in a field
Drunk with diabolical sacraments,
Shrieks of all tormented by invisible hands
And miraculous visions. Salem trials.

So the raven flag, the castle and the lion
Rose, lily banners, the orange white and blue
Hauled up the Half Moon in from Amsterdam,
And the red cross on white, white cross on blue,
The Union Jack, the English Meteor flew;
Pine trees and rattlesnakes, Colonial rebels
Cut out the cantons on the village square:

And Franklin played with lightning and the French.
Washington shaped a land out of Valley Forge.

3

There are two New Englands, north and south:
Maine, Vermont, New Hampshire form the one,
Connecticut, Rhode Island, Massachusetts,
The other.
               Colors of all seasons: the salt
Marshes, maples on the inland hills

In autumn, the long-shadowed winter,
Yellow spring and the heavy fruit and shade
Of summer: cranberries and marble,
Red cherry limbs, the lusty Merrimac
Draining the stingy soil out of New England.

West of New England, the fingers of placid lakes;
There's Troy and Rome, Utica, Syracuse,
Niagara, broken bottomland, Lily Dale,
Millerite, Chautauqua, Shaker, Shinnecock,
Land of Yankee Doodle and Rip Van,
Vassar, island of fire, sing sing New York!

Newcastle, Kent and Sussex, Delaware
Of duco lucite dacron cellophane—names
Milled by the willows on the Brandywine,
Clan of the admirable admiral.

Pennsylvania, America's friend:
Pittsburgh Gettysburg Hershey's chocolate bars
Ingots and blooms, electric boats and bears,
Germantown, Chestnut Hill and Seven Stars.

New Jersey, island of the Delaware—
Passaic Paterson Hudson's Palisades—
Slave of two cities bursts like a rose.

Empire state of the South, of rococola,
Coosa and Tallapoosa. Georgia booze
Grows hair on Brasstown Bald. Drink Coca-Cola

In Maryland east on Chesapeake Bay
The Chester Choptank Nanticoke Pocomoke rivers

Roll red and yellow. West to Wills Mountain,
The Appalachian Ridge; Antietam Creek
And Conococheague wind south to the Potomac;
Great Cumberland, the Piedmont, Sugar Loaf—
All testimonials to Baltimore.

South Carolina: sectional
Lowland and upland, hinterland and salt
Palmetto beaches, herons and hemlocks.

North Carolina: intellectual
Of Black and Blue Ridge Mountains, Hairy Bear,
Dismal Swamp, sound of the Albermarle.

Virginia, bright Virginia: daring Byrds
And brilliant Glass, apple aristocrat.

West Virginia, little Switzerland,
Charleston on the Kanawha, Koppers, raw
Star of synthetics, Wheeling of steel.

4

Maine and Vermont, mountain and maple.

From the Yadkin to Kentucky Daniel Boone
Opened the wilderness into Tennessee:

White Oak and Chickamauga, Tennessee
Is ridge and river, scarp and rolling plain,
Reelfoot, Cumberland, Big Monday mules.

Bluegrass and moonshine, possum and raccoon:

Heaven is Kentucky. Pennyrile and knobs.

Porcelain and peonies, an empire within
An empire, of Napoleon, Greasy Ridge,
Timken roller bearings, nuts and bolts,
Derricks and cranes, Buckeye wheelbarrows:
Ohio's deeper boom runs everywhere.

Indiana chimneys and yellow corn:
Hoosierland—sand, soil and light.

Oxbow and bayou, loblollies oaks
Cotton and indigo, azaleas, Rose
Of Mississippi, Natchez in decay.

Alabama: Tuskegee's trees,
Chickasaws Choctaws Creeks and Cherokees,
Coosa, Raccoon and Lookout, Little mountains.

Herculean Illinois and the dinosaur
Of cities: King of the Bombers Schemer Bugs
And thugs—Urbana Rockford Elgin Bloom-
ington East St. Louis Chicagoans
Hinky Dink, Bathhouse John and Scarface Al.

Detroit men with the millimeter gauge
Are Michigan's fishermen. River Rouge,
Willow Run, mercurial juggernauts.

Manitowok, Sheboygan, melting pot
Of Germans Poles Norwegians Swiss and Danes:
Oshkosh Kenosha Neehah Green Bay—craft
Of Kraft and Kleenex, Borden's Badger State.

5

Missouri, little Dixie state of the saints
(Louis Charles Joseph Francois Genevieve)
Boonslick and Ozark, Taum Sauk, Pilot Knob.

> *St. Louis rose on timber, brick and stone,*
> *Bellefontaine south to Carondelet,*
> *Grew to the west, setting of steel and glass,*
> *Seed of all settlement, womb of the West.*

Louisiana: Creole and Cajun,
Noblesse of Negro, corn and Carnival.

Sweet Home and Hot Springs, chinchillas, Lake
Hamilton, melons of Hope, diamonds, straw-
berries, Ozarks and orchids—Arkansas.

Strawland oatland cornbelt Iowa hogs
("Corn makes 'em fat, it's oats that make 'em grow")

Port of Duluth, sea-fronting, swollen blue
Country of Astor, Sieur du Lhut, the Sioux,
The Chippewa, tamarack twist of the gray Mesabi,
Glaciers and gladioli, purple ore.

Heart of America Kansas, people of the south
Wind, out of New England and the South,
They came with Beecher's Bibles, buffalo
Hunters preachers abolitionists came,
Nation of Carry and Curry bleeding, one
Track of the Osage, Pike's Route, Oregon,
Lem Blanchard and the jayhawk yellow as the sun-
flower, yellow as corn and Turkey wheat.

And out of Nebraska William Jennings Bryan
Came, out of flat water country, railroad land
Of dusty Omaha, cornhusker city of men.

Colorado cradled potash padishahs,
Barons of sugar-beets, margraves of mines.
Big Thompson and Blue River, Gunnison
Tunnel through the Divide, irrigate
And make the prairie bloom, O columbine!

North Dakota, flickertail, inflamed
Whirlpool of semolina flour and wheat,
Sentinel Butte and Killdeer, Cannonball.

South Dakota, heart and soul of the great
Plain of the world: Bad Lands Black Hills Sioux Falls
Red and White Rivers Rushmore Borglum busts
Spearfish and Owl, chukar partridges.

Montana—it's "bigger than Italy"—
Of Wheelers dealers Anacondas and Hel-
ena's hot afternoons
                        Golcondas bawdy Butte
Custer Copperopolis and the Scratch-
Gravel Mountains, Molly Muck-a-Chuck
And Buttermilk Jim, Black Eagle, Hungry Horse
Sunburst gazoonis sapphires in the mud.

Down to the land of trails, the Oregon
Mormon Bridger's Bozeman Overland
Here where the rivers rise and flow to the west
And south: the Snake, North Platte and Yellowstone,
Rectangular Wyoming. O Jackson Hole!

Oklahoma: Five Civilized Tribes
By whom all things were given, even the land.

6

Florida: Big Cypress, Apalachicola,
Okeechobee and Okefenokee,
The circus, the citrus and the Seminole.

7

The Spaniards brought hide, hoofs and horns, longhorns,
Then shorthorns, hornless Anguses ran the range,
Santa Gertrudis, Texas strawberries.

(New Mexico's where Mr. Coronado
Ate corn-on-the-cob and bears have corkscrew tails
So they can sit without sliding into Texas.)

8

Rogue and Coquille, Burnt, Powder—rivers run
The Snake-edged state of the beaver Oregon
Of Klamath, Mount Mazama's Crater Lake.

Seattle to Spokane, the slopes of wheat,
Copper and fawn, emerald tumbleweeds,
Wenatchee red-cheeked apples, Walla Walla,
Rainier, Olympus, coulees and cascades.

Sandpoint to Pocatello, Idaho falls:
Moscow to Paris, Bear and Bitter Root
Lo Lo Clearwater Craters of the Moon.

9

California had men to match her mountains:
Cortez, Juan Rodriguez Cabrillo searched
For seven golden cities never found;
Fremont, Tom Larkin, Sutter and King (James)
Civilized a land of barbarous names:
Hangtown Puke Ravine Hell's Delight
Gouge Eye Brandy Gulch Petticoat Slide.

Deseret Utah and the living God,
Driven to the desert, Mormon pioneers,
The twelve apostles lean and bearded gray.

Naughty Nevada: Reno Tonopah
Towns of roulette and faro, slot machines
Lost Wages
          O bonanza! Comstock Lode

Arizona: Pimas, Penitentes,
The risen phoenix, tombstone epitaph.

10

Jump off to Juneau, sniff the Klondike air.
Chilkat Kodiak Katmai fumaroles
Barrow to Ketchikan, Aleutian chain,
Triangle of islands, panhandle, plateau;
Bering to Yukon, sedimented gold,
Salmon and spruce, walrus and wolverine,
Offshoots, Aleuts, Alaskan Eskimos!

11

Hilo to Honolulu and Niihau,
Green plains of Kaneohe, mynah birds
Chirp in the flame trees, banyans, coconuts:
Hawaii is aloha, holiday,
Head of a diamond, heart of a pearl.

12

Now men go weightless, fixed by the same star
That guided the mariner out of San Lucar,
And separate from the land, the forgotten land;
Blind to the rising headlands, the soft rain
Falling on the savannahs, the singing wind-
gaps in the Alleghenies, the long sundown
Hung high in the dusty plains, spikes of flame,
Snowplants in the Sierras and the black
Sands of Kalapana, the prairies choked with sand:

Remember the land, remember the land.

Birdcatcher

A flight bending
the reeds of
easy ponds seeks
asylum in the
cold horizon.

Under the noisy
flock a birdcatcher
trumpets but a
farther distance
calls them, an inner
wind torments them,
they weave unknowing
the tightest net
where feathers disappear,
from first to last
the sky lifts at
their isosceles
advance: a breathlessness
of birds.

Birdkeeper

Birds birds . . . "Mister, do you keep birds?"
a passing boy had asked, and I might have answered,
"No, birds keep me." That was closer to the truth,
though we can't say we've given each other life,
but since I kept so many birds alive,
our lives together, they owed me the life
of these lines; I hadn't praised or reproached them,
or feared or punished them in ancestral ways
of superstition and strange amulets,
only indulged them beyond what nature meant
for them: the crippled mockingbird that flew
to greet us, alighted, suspended a frozen claw
and always took three raisins from our palm,
the catbird that took an uninvited seat
on our shoulders; sparrows, fat pure-blooded heirs
of pairs set free in Pennsylvania
or brought into St. Louis by Henry Shaw
that spawned into these fantastic chattering hordes
but kept the manners of gentlefolk; and jays,
crows, mourning doves, an occasional hawk.
                                        For you
a passing boy once asked, "Do you keep birds,
mister?" Spontaneous answer, "No,
they hold me prisoner!" But he'd have walked away
puzzled. Now like the hours and days I gave them
they've disappeared into a late winter sun.

Beau

—dead of feline leukemia

Named for a general Beau-
regard the handsome one

with great triangular jaw
black bushy tail

and pure white breast and throat
you commanded a home for a year

imperious as a khan
knowing what pharaohs knew

nursed for two fortnights
as if our own lives hung

on the balance of your breath
we fought the vile disease

that violated your blood
and burned away your youth

You came in our winter lives
and died on the edge of spring.

Good Neighbor

The only time I spoke to Albert Walker
he was slumped in his car with a crumpled ten-dollar bill

between his legs. His chin was on his chest,
arms at his sides, eyes closed, and I knew right away

he was sleeping; but I knocked on the closed window.
"Are you all right?" But he didn't answer,

and then I saw the beer cans on the floor
behind the seat and I knew he had passed out.

I ran in the house and called the police
three times in ten minutes. I called the police

and asked for an ambulance. When the police came
I gave them a coat hanger to open the door

and it took ten minutes to open the locked door
and the fumes rushed out. It was a hot morning.

They shook his body and it was stiff; and I knew
he had been dead since yesterday afternoon

in plain sight on a busy boulevard,
counting his day's receipts. There might have been more

to all this than the curious neighbors knew,
magnetized in a horde around the five

police cars, the van, the ambulance and the hearse.
As the mailman said the next day, "It might have been worse,

he might have suffered." But why was he there
on the passenger side, sealed in so hot and still?

The only time I spoke to Albert Walker
he was slumped in his car with a crumpled ten-dollar bill.

Triptych Written at a
Myra Cohn Livingston Lecture

1

Among the oaks dead or dying, one
rattles in the winter sky where a man, a runner
remembers its green in the woods, or under its sleep
as a skater, where its branches now
are frozen, black swallows over a vanished pond.

2

What if I were this dead or dying
oak, rattling in the winter sky? . . . A man
must remember his green, a runner
in the woods, with the grass or the crisp
leaves underfoot; but now I'm only
this frozen limb where the black
swallows alight over the vanished pond.

3

You are this dead or dying oak, a man
rattling in the winter sky but remembering
the green of the woods with grass or autumn leaves
underfoot; and when the oak slept you skated
here where you stand frozen now, limbs,
black swallows over a vanished pond.

Beginnings

The past is gone, the future hasn't come,
the present slips away: do we depend
on nothing? Nothing answers, for it is dumb
and nothing has no beginning and no end.
For the time has come when the suffering of the root
becomes the root of suffering and the tree
of wisdom, bare of its customary fruit,
loses its image of abundancy.

And the time has come when the reason for desire
is tempered and the desire for reason
explodes from ashes into continuous fire
of light and heat against the severe season,
and in the meditation of the flame,
beyond the one sensation that it warms,
we perceive the function of its dancing game
and recognize the clarity of its forms;

until the time has come when the change of light
yields to the light of change, music of space
played in the half dark of an elusive night
of alternate despair and silent grace,
seeming to drown the time when the rest of being
ends and being at rest suddenly draws near,
when the sight of birds vanishes and the bird of seeing
flies away somewhere else, away from here.

Hummingbirds

Hummingbirds: airmen
of luminous moss and ferns
whirred in the mist, grace.

Elements

I think

all circles

gathering the world,

I gather earth

air fire water

and in the beginning

discover a fifth

element

arching over and

moving

the seasons

Liccle Sorrel

(for Al Lewis)

I'll never forget when I cut him out of the string,
bridled him in the corral, led him out
to the rig, dropped the saddle, wrapped the cinch
ring on his belly, gentle old cow-
horse, wooled him around a bit, gave him
a few light kicks in the paunch then swung aboard;
well-reined, he could turn on a dime and we range-
branded all morning and he didn't roll an eye.

So I took him in to water him and leaned
to slap his neck when he watched me like a hawk.
Kinky old plug, he snuffed and suddenly
dropped an ear, crow-hopped, humped, then pitched and pitched;
I pulled all the leather I could but we broke in two
and I dragged him back to camp with dirty hands.

Three Balloons / Flowers

On a portrait by Malinowski

Heat, light and air surround this girl or else
spring from her: red, yellow, blue. Balloons or flowers?
Only a hand implies a body; the face
is a flower, teeth-petaled, brow-styled.

Her eyes hold hurricanes
and suns simultaneously, calm
and chaos: might rock landslide-
like, or in smile burst, suddenly.

Six Picassos, One Ernst

The Acrobats (PICASSO)

A fat man A frail boy
He heavy in wisdom He light in sin
Struck a rose and blue
Attitude on a box

Did this horned man
Procreate
That sky-haired nude
Innocence
Thin as it is
And will the red creature hold
for all plainly to see
The clear flesh in his grasp
And spoil it by his will?

Still Life with Skull and Leeks (PICASSO)

With its own smell
Of decay long gone
This skull
Grins at the living
Pitcher The leeks
Lying unaired
By the locked window give
A new energy of death
To this cheekless

Dora Maar: Three Portraits (PICASSO)

The cow the bull
The vegetable

Bare flesh strong
Nostrils and water-
melon breast

The last
Red and green striped
Torso and glad
Face depressed

Two Figures (PICASSO)

Inscrutably
Weary and depressed
With secrets
Of love and poverty

They sit (unable
Perhaps even to buy
One drink one pipeful)
Blue and blue against blue

And stay
Far into morning
Until the café closes
And they must build their own fire

Clarinet Player (PICASSO)

Green notes sounded
Downdraft in a
Slimy well
                    Drawn
A deep song

But I'm in that well
Those mossy blocks
Aren't real Over me
There's a yellow mouth
Of a man who fingers
The keys
            And beckons
Consummate music

The Mirror (PICASSO)

Her glass repeats
Face to face
Full
Profiled
Belly and breasts
Ovally
Doubled
The glass with her
Foretelling age
In gray
Blue purple
But the womb
Is green

Portrait (MAX ERNST)

More flesh than eyes
Blue flesh
Volleys of motion
Her body ordered
As a bird stretched
In mist

And the print
Of bottle and bouquet

Buds of laughing and
Eyes quenched
In a wall of day

Twelve Pettisongs

Schooner (FEININGER)

Flowing umber
topsail in precise
angles cleaving
blue and yellow

Loners (PAUL KLEE)

Only two
but not together
rather
walking alone into the dark
blue to the vivid sun

Birdcatcher (PAUL KLEE)

O the plumes
pink blue green
orange yellow brown
in a setting
of blood

Naked (MODIGLIANI)

Oval
shoulders broad
hips
red purple black
fleshed lips

Girl (MODIGLIANI)

Four-letter words:
look   wish   love   girl

Mother/Child (PICASSO)

Rosy brown mother
chestnut child
                    Was Jesus
white?

Pierrot (PICASSO)

How the frail white-
costumed flesh in black
hat and pumps
quarrels with the dark
red green and brown
for dominion

Vase/Flowers (PICASSO)

Can the flowers be more beautiful
than the vase
apparent in permanence
as a flashing swallow
blooms?

Bathers (RENOIR)

Shimmering raw
fawn-fleshed
trio

Clown (RENOIR)

My flesh
as clown:
pink and blue
joy among animals
clawing the sawdust

Boy (RUBENS)

Pouting flushed
plump with dreams
still the encumbered
flesh of his mother

Sunflowers (VAN GOGH)

Corps of yellow
green-yellow
brown
green
An attack of sunflowers

Hero

Near this spot a hundred and ten
years ago a man named Whitey
Walker and his family
(wife, three boys, two girls)
died they say of thirst
or maybe exposure, huddled
together in the hot and cold
desert air.
            And the wolves
picked them bare and even
the bones at last disappeared.

Now there's a new hamburger
house and the young jacks,
schoolboys down from Las Vegas,
pull aside in their Mustangs
every afternoon for milk
shakes cokes
and 68 flavors of ice cream
consumed in cool
air with stereo music;

or at a drive-in draw
up in pairs, squealing,
lifting the dust as their pony
cars peel out on the freeway,
playing chancier games where

the hero chicken loses
neck, guts and cock-
les—and the whole faculty
and student body mourn him and the high
school band plays at his funeral.

Another Year

Hungary: a boy
stunted in his play
of climbing in the beeches,
whistling in the streets.

Hungary: a girl
never under freedom,
pleasing a new master,
old before her time.

Hungary: a man
strong with old desires,
sweating in the factory,
laboring in the fields.

Hungary: a woman
watching at her window,
waiting for a lover
who never comes.

The Water Bill

I dreamed that the reason so many European
and American poets wrote about water bills
was that Jouve had mentioned one in one of his poems.
I got up and looked
through *Mélodrame* and all the anthologies
but there wasn't a word about any water bill.
Not one.
           There was only a fat planet
turning, supporting its night waters,
a lake among mountains, dark lakes
of eyes moved by love and eyes
tormented by fire, oceans of eyes, and leaves
turned crystal after the rain, yellow obituaries
of familiar poets, swans dying of thirst.
Then I went outside:
it was dark, the paper wasn't there, nothing
was flowing, the neighbors weren't home
or their cars. Even the dogs
were gone.

Wide River

Born in a drop on a frozen mountainside,
Rushing in forks from the Platte to the Yellowstone,
Its fury and peace are lost in the ocean tide.

Where the lark, the curlew, eagle and heron cried
And the bison grazed with the pinto and wild roan,
Born in a drop on a frozen mountainside,

Tumbling through hills where the bear and pronghorn hide,
In prairie floods or a sun that burns to the bone,
Its fury and peace are lost in the ocean tide.

Where the keelboat and the mackinaw used to glide
By the trail of Parkman, Shaw and Chatillon,
Born in a drop on a frozen mountainside,

It furrowed the plains where the Crow and Dakota ride
To Wounded Knee where Yellow Bird stood alone . . .
(Its fury and peace are lost in the ocean tide.)

At Beaver Creek and the Washita they died,
Now the rifle and bow together lie overgrown.
Born in a drop on a frozen mountainside,
Its fury and peace are lost in the ocean tide.

World of Fun

Everything's possible from the Johnson Smith
Catalog: everything's made easy with the electronic lie
and love detector, the police handcuffs you can snap
over the Hercules wristband and escape
if you wish by the secrets of 15 baffling tricks
revealed in the 24-page book; the cane will dance
for you, the key will bend, the skeleton
glow, the handkerchief burn with the secret thumb;
do the waterfall shuffle with the Electric Deck,
tell all with the de luxe fortune-telling Predicta Board;
get smart, learn while you sleep, develop a winning
personality, overcome your enemies & hidden fears
with the Seven Keys to Power used by ancient priests,
kings and mystics. Moneyback guarantee.

For 150 $$$ you can buy a gorilla
suit with a gory mask and cause howls of laughter.
Big Ear and Super Phones and the Pocket Electronic
Blackjack Computer: split stand draw
and automatic bust; or do some impossible thing
with the Pocket Miracle Scientific Walking Spring
(nothing to wind, walks lifelike in your hands!)
Fun from the sun with miniature solar cells,
a sun-powered beany from your plastic hat,
104 easy gadgets you can build!
Last Supper tablecloths, the de luxe bottle
cutter, the pocket Metal Detector & Money Finder
to make you rich! 3000 colorful Indian
beads, silver enamel, liquid gold.

Turn light into current; virtually unlimited
life. No batteries needed. Unlimited life.

II

R E F O R M A T I O N S

"Reformations implies more than translating or adapting poems from another language. It suggests a higher degree of respect for the original text and author."

The Clown

The stage a lively band is shaking rumbles
Under the clumsy-footed clown who flouts
(Not without skill and haughtiness) the louts
Stomping the boards up front and whom he humbles.

His painted cheeks are marvelous! He mumbles,
Then stops as suddenly as he puffs and shouts,
And roguishly receives quick kicks and clouts,
Pecks at his plump companion's neck, then tumbles.

Let's heartily applaud his claptrap speech!
His short, flowered vest and nimble limbs that reach
And twist deceptively are worth the view;

But most of all we like that wig, perched high
Upon his head, with its long dangling queue
Trailed by a swiftly fluttering butterfly.

—from the French of Paul Verlaine (1844-1896)

For a Long Time You Held . . .

(for khalam)

For a long time you held the soldier's black face in your hands
As if some fatal sundown already shone upon it.
From the hill I watched the sun go down in the bays of your eyes.
When will I see my land again, the clear skyline of your face?
When will I sit down again at the table of your sullen breast?

And the nest of sweet talk is in half darkness.

I'll see other skies and other eyes
I'll drink at the spring of other mouths cooler than citrons
I'll sleep under the roofs of other hair sheltered from storms.
But every year when the rum of spring sets fire to my memory
I'll miss my homeland and the rain of your eyes
    on the thirsty savannas.

—from the French of Léopold Sédar Senghor (b. 1906)

Black Stone
On a White Stone

I'll die in Paris during a thunderstorm
on a day which even now I can recall
I'll die in Paris—but I'm not concerned—
maybe some Thursday like today, in the fall.

It will be Thursday, for as I write these lines
today my arms and shoulders feel sore,
and I have never felt as I feel now,
in all my days, more lonely than before.

César Vallejo's dead; they clubbed him down,
everyone, though he never did them harm,
everyone beat him hard with clubs and beat

him hard with a rope; the only witnesses
were Thursdays and the arm and shoulder bones,
the solitude, the highways and the storm.

—from the Spanish of César Vallejo (1894-1937)

In Prison . . .

In prison at Genoa
Marco made his point
Now truth is embarrassing
They didn't believe him at all.

You'd have had to conceal
The pearls in his pouches
For the earth was round
And the lakes were oceans.

The things I tell
Are veritable lies
But I'd die of shame
If you found it out.

—*from the French of Jean Cocteau* (1887-1963)

Silenτ Game

I caught life
With my teeth
On the knife
Of my youth.
Today with my lips,
Only my lips

A brief upstart,
The hillside flower,
Orion's spear
Has reappeared.

—from the French of René Char (1907-1988)

Tell Me If You Remember, Love

Tell me if you remember, love,
those tender, lazy
yellow reeds
that lay in the dry ditch.

Do you remember the poppy
that summer pulverized,
the withered poppy,
black crepe over the prairie?

Do you remember the morning sun,
low and motionless,
shining and trembling, broken
on a frozen fountain?

—from the Spanish of Antonio Machado (1875-1939)

What Do You Want, Shepherd of Wind?

And there's still the call of the old
shepherd's horn, harsh over the white
ditches of snakeskins. Perhaps
it gives breath to the plains of Acquaviva,
where the Platani rolls sea-shells
under the water between the feet of young
olive-skinned boys. O as for earth the gust
of imprisoned wind breaks and echoes
in the already crumbling light; what do you want,
shepherd of wind? Perhaps you summon the dead.
You do not hear with me, confused by the sea's
reverberation, attentive to the low cry
of fishermen lifting their nets.

—*from the Italian of Salvatore Quasimodo* (1901-1968)

On an Unwritten Letter

Is it for tingling sunrises, for a few
strands on which the tuft
of life is tangled and strung out
in hours and years that dolphins somersault
in pairs with their young today? Oh that I'd hear
nothing of you, that I could escape the flash
of your eyes. There are other things on earth.

I can't disappear or reappear; the vermilion
furnace of night is late
and evening lingers on;
prayer is torture and not yet
among the rising rocks has the bottle
reached you from the sea. The waves
break emptily on the cape at Finisterre.

—from the Italian of Eugenio Montale (1896-1981)

Posthumous

We must give the dead everyday speech,
Words which pass easily from our lips to their ears,
Words to keep us company
When we're no longer alive.
Help me, men, my friends,
It's not a job for one alone,
With these common phrases polished by time,
Your speech and mine as well as our fathers'
Especially for the war dead
With their careers blown up,
Phrases chosen with care
To give them assurance.
Nothing is more afraid than a dead man
If he feels the outside air a little
That leaves him suspicious
Phrases we must hold ready
So they can move their lips
And finding them beautiful for having served so long
They feel the slight fever
Of one who once lost the memory of darkness
And looks ahead.

—from the French of Jules Supervielle (1884-1960)